C000146532

the little book of
SPIRITUALITY

lucy lane

summersdale

THE LITTLE BOOK OF SPIRITUALITY

Copyright © Summersdale Publishers Ltd, 2018

Text by Vicky Edwards

Candle icon © Blan-k/Shutterstock.com

An Hachette UK Company
www.hachette.co.uk

Summersdale Publishers Ltd
Part of Octopus Publishing Group Limited
Carmelite House
50 Victoria Embankment
LONDON
EC4Y 0DZ
UK

www.summersdale.com

Printed and bound in the Czech Republic

ISBN: 978-1-78685-517-6

Substantial discounts on bulk quantities of Summersdale books are available to corporations, professional associations and other organisations. For details contact general enquiries: telephone: +44 (0) 1243 771107 or email: enquiries@summersdale.com.

For Moira

INTRODUCTION

Modern-day spirituality is a quest for personal development and a more enlightened existence. It is not concerned with the value of material things, but with core values such as altruism, integrity and compassion. Whether your journey is inspired by faith or the pursuit of spiritual fulfilment, this handy little book is packed with inspiring quotations and simple tips to help you – it's a tool-kit to support you on your way to serenity.

GET TO KNOW YOUR SPIRITUAL SELF

Spirituality is a personal journey where we try to establish and nurture a connection with something greater than ourselves. To do this, we must first look to ourselves: at our beliefs, our values and our actions. What could you change or improve upon? Based on your life to date, create an honest personal moral inventory. Explore your character traits, ideals and beliefs, especially around the themes of fairness, integrity and love, and acknowledge your strengths as well as your weaknesses.

The following questions will help you discover your core values and create your moral inventory:

- What are my positive and negative qualities?
- Do I have a belief system?
- Are there outstanding apologies or amends I need to make to myself or others that would give me greater peace of mind?
- What resentments am I carrying that it would benefit me to let go?

This truthful moral inventory provides a sound basis from which to begin your journey to enlightenment.

KNOWING YOURSELF IS THE BEGINNING OF ALL WISDOM.

Aristotle

Grant me the serenity
to accept the things
I cannot change,
the courage to change
the things I can,
and the wisdom to
know the difference.

Reinhold Niebuhr

BE MINDFUL

The objective of mindfulness is to learn how to cope with your emotions without feeling overwhelmed by them. Focusing on the here and now is an effective means of achieving a state of calm. Try sitting quietly, closing your eyes and concentrating on steady breathing. Stop your mind from darting about and let the natural rhythm of your breath guide your way. If your mind wanders, gently bring it back to the task in hand.

Another helpful mindfulness exercise is to take a deep breath and then slowly exhale. Concentrate on that outward breath and ask yourself if it feels as if it is carrying any particular emotion. If the answer is yes, identify the emotion and observe it simply by name – fear, anger, sadness. Don't attempt to discover its origin or to justify it; just calmly sit with it. Experts in psychology claim that by specifically labelling an emotion that troubles us we decrease its intensity.

The **pursuit**, even
of the best things,
ought to be **calm**
and **tranquil**.

Marcus Tullius Cicero

IF YOU WANT TO CONQUER THE ANXIETY OF LIFE, LIVE IN THE MOMENT, LIVE IN THE BREATH.

Amit Ray

CHALLENGE ACCEPTED

When the going gets tough, a state of acceptance can be difficult to maintain. Emotions such as anger, indignation and denial can scupper any sense of serenity that we might have. Likewise, having to accept what we perceive as the unacceptable can make our blood boil to the point that we are incapable of all reason. Instead, try to see that a situation simply 'is', rather than 'is wrong/unfair'.

Acceptance doesn't mean rolling over and taking whatever comes our way, good or bad. Ultimately, acceptance is about seeking a more peaceful and productive way forward, without being distracted by negative and unconstructive emotions. When our mental capacity is unclouded we are in a stronger position to be objective and practical.

A journey of a
thousand miles begins
with a single step.

Lao Tzu

In every day, there are
1,440 minutes.
That means we
have 1,440 daily
opportunities to
make a positive impact.

Les Brown

THINK POSITIVE

Emotional health and spiritual balance require a positive state of mind, so cultivate a 'can do' mindset until it becomes instinctive. Practising positivity, especially towards others, diminishes negative emotions such as hate, envy and jealousy and leaves your mind and heart clearer and lighter. Be willing and ready to seek out silver linings even in the darkest of situations.

Make a conscious decision to stay alert for negative thoughts and be ready to challenge them whenever they pop into your head. If they do, try a mindful exercise like visualising your negativity being carried away on the breeze and out of your sight.

Choose your company wisely: if you know someone to be a doomsayer who always steals your sunshine, give them a wide berth. Or be prepared to call them out on their habit of always seeing the glass as half empty. People can only drain your positivity if you allow them to.

The **first step** toward change is **awareness**. The second step is **acceptance**.

Nathaniel Branden

What you need is to
recognise the possibilities
and challenges offered
by the present moment,
and to embrace them.

Thomas Merton

GIVE YOURSELF PERMISSION TO FAIL

Failure is one of the most useful lessons we can learn: it shapes our next attempt, making us aware of where the pitfalls are and what we need to do better. Fear of failure is the most common reason people give for not doing something, and yet in not doing it they are failing without even trying!

Failure teaches us much more than success does – remember that the likes of Steve Jobs and Thomas Edison built their careers and their business empires on the back of their failures in so far as their early efforts taught them what *didn't* work. When we pick ourselves back up, having learned from our mistakes, the taste of success when it comes is all the sweeter. To fail is to learn. To learn is to be closer to triumph and spiritual enlightenment.

THE PHOENIX MUST BURN TO EMERGE.

Janet Fitch

Our **greatest glory** is not in never falling, but in **rising** every time we fall.

Oliver Goldsmith

ESCAPE YOUR COMFORT ZONE

Most of us avoid stepping outside our comfort zones for fear of failure at some level. In order to develop spiritually, we sometimes need to take a leap of faith to go beyond the limits we set ourselves. If you know this is something you struggle with, start small. You'll be surprised by how quickly you can go from making steady steps to bolder leaps.

Initiate the awkward conversation that you are dreading; apply for the job you feel underqualified for; introduce yourself to strangers who might become your allies. Try to find something every day that gives you the opportunity to push yourself. It will boost your confidence and nourish your spirit.

It is not that we do not
dare because things are
difficult; it is because
we do not dare that
they are difficult.

Seneca

A SHIP IN A HARBOUR IS SAFE – BUT THAT IS NOT WHAT SHIPS ARE BUILT FOR.

John A. Shedd

START AS YOU MEAN TO GO ON

Start every day with a moment of reflection. Even if you don't pray or meditate, a short time spent focusing on how you intend to face the day ahead can bring great clarity and set you up to achieve your goals and objectives. Aim to be the very best possible version of yourself that you can be.

Make each day your
masterpiece.

John Wooden

ORGANISED CHAOS

It is almost impossible to feel a spiritual connection to anything if you are living in chaos. If you have a tendency to create mess, make a concerted effort to be neater; put things away, clean up after yourself as you go and keep on top of domestic chores. A tidy environment is reflective: tidy home, tidy mind. There is also something soothing and rhythmic about tidying and cleaning, so the act itself can be beneficial to our spiritual health and sense of contentment.

Learning is the beginning of spirituality. Searching and learning is where the miracle process all begins.

Jim Rohn

LIFE HAS
A WAY OF
SETTING THINGS
IN ORDER AND
LEAVING THEM
BE. VERY TIDY,
IS LIFE.

Jean Anouilh

Organising is what
you do before you do
something, so that
when you do it, it is
not all mixed up.

a. a. Milne

JOURNEY WITH A JOURNAL

Keep a hand-written spiritual journal. There is something in physically writing (as opposed to typing) that creates more powerful connections between mind, body and spirit. Invest in a good-quality notebook and a pen that you find easy to write or sketch with so that your journaling is a pleasant experience. Empty your heart and soul into its pages and note your feelings, your triumphs and your struggles.

Resolve to write at a similar time each day, so that expressing yourself on the page becomes part of your routine. Try to be as descriptive as you can in recording your spiritual and emotional temperature. If words are difficult to come up with, draw how you feel. Take time to look back now and again, observing any patterns in thought or behaviour that you need to work on.

JOURNAL WRITING IS A VOYAGE TO THE INTERIOR.

Christina Baldwin

Writing in a journal...
offers a place where you
can hold a deliberate,
thoughtful conversation
with yourself.

Robin Sharma

DIGITAL DETOX

Although technology is an integral part of daily life, try to find time each week when you can detach from all digital paraphernalia. Switch off your phone and all other devices and relish the freedom it brings. Reducing our interaction with the digital world reduces stress and enables us to step back to re-evaluate, refocus and reconnect with loved ones. Instead of frittering an hour away on social media, do something unrelated to technology that you enjoy but haven't done for ages. Do what you love instead of looking for 'likes'.

Bedtime is a good daily point to disconnect. The light from screens stops production of the hormone melatonin, which is vital for getting to sleep, so log out of devices at least two hours before you go to bed and make your bedroom a tech-free zone. Instead of reading emails, read an inspirational book or practise mindfulness. At least twice a year take a digital detox holiday. Even a long weekend without logging on will help clear your head and improve your connection with the cosmos.

Radiate peace. Who knows? The peace you spread may create the only restful place in your environment.

Stella Payton

BE THE CALM CENTRE IN THE RAGING FLOW OF LIFE.

Leo Babauta

STARTING OVER

It's easy to let something upsetting dictate your mood or attitude for the rest of the day. When this happens, get into the habit of beginning your day again and make a conscious decision to return to a place of calm. Even if it is last thing at night, say out loud, 'I am starting my day again' and reclaim your equilibrium.

Yesterday is the past,
tomorrow is the
future, but today is a
gift. That is why it is
called the present.

Bil Keane

DO THE ROUTINE RHUMBA

As creatures of habit, we tend to do most regular tasks in exactly the same way. The routes we walk, our ablutions, meals, working practices – we are as regular as proverbial clockwork. By mixing things up we become more observant and alert. Step outside your well-practised routines and see if the universe delivers any surprises as a result.

Changing the way you
do **routine** things
allows a **new person**
to grow inside of you.

Paulo Coelho

TIME FOR TAO

Taoism as a discipline has its origins in ancient China: Lao Tzu, a prominent sage of the sixth century BCE, is credited as its founder. '*Tao*' is loosely translated as 'the way', and this spiritual tradition is based on the belief that there is a single all-pervading energy, known as *chi*, guiding everything along its path. True *tao* cannot be articulated, but felt only by becoming attuned to nature and achieving harmony with the rhythms of the universe.

The objective of Taoism is to experience life in an effortless way and therefore to keep energy flowing when you need it. An important principle is 'action through inaction'. Known as *wu wei*, this involves understanding the flow of energy around you and therefore the optimum time for action – when to act and when to relax. In your everyday life, carefully consider the moments when not acting on a thought or feeling may be more beneficial to you in the long run.

Trying to understand is like straining through muddy water. Have the patience to wait! Be still and allow the mud to settle.

Lao Tzu

THE MOON DOES NOT FIGHT. IT ATTACKS NO ONE. IT DOES NOT WORRY. IT DOES NOT TRY TO CRUSH OTHERS.

Ming-Dao Deng

BE MORE
LIKE BUDDHA

Buddhists pursue the spiritual state of enlightenment through practices such as meditation, reflection and rituals. They follow the path of the Buddha, Siddhartha Gautama, who began his own quest for enlightenment some time in the sixth or fifth century BCE. Buddhism is best seen as a philosophy rather than a religion, as Buddhists do not worship deities.

Buddhism teaches that nothing is fixed, and that change is always possible. Its major insight is that human suffering is caused by our belief that things can last and our craving for things to be a certain way. Only when we let go of such cravings can we truly be happy.

In practical terms, Buddhism is a flexible belief system that may be applied to everyday life. Although it is an ancient philosophy, it has much to offer in a modern world where speed, achievement and conspicuous consumption are highly prized.

LOOK INTO LU JONG

Meaning 'body transformation' in Tibetan, Lu Jong is a form of yoga that may help balance the mind and ease emotional ills. It claims to combine methods of movement and breathing to free blockages in the flow of energy through your body. Although it is a practice most commonly transmitted through oral teachings, a number of resources can be found online if the idea of Lu Jong appeals to you.

A **calm mind** is
not disturbed by the
waves of thoughts.

Remez Sasson

Acquire inner peace and
a multitude will find
their salvation near you.

Catherine de Hueck Doherty

IF I KEEP A
GREEN BOUGH IN
MY HEART, THEN
THE SINGING
BIRD WILL COME.

Chinese proverb

TRY T'AI CHI

T'ai chi is a Chinese martial art that offers a multitude of health benefits, including longevity, relaxation, improved balance and greater self-awareness. Rooted in the practice of moderation and self-control, t'ai chi encourages discipline of the mind and body to create a type of 'moving meditation'.

Linked to many principles of traditional Chinese medicine, t'ai chi training also helps the joints by exercising them through moves that require relaxation rather than muscular tension. The slow and repetitive process is said to increase internal circulation, which over time brings about a remarkable reversal of the physical effects of stress. With this achieved, you can then utilise your 'spare' energy and a clear head to focus on more spiritual pursuits.

With the **gentlest** movements of t'ai chi comes the **quieting** of emotions.

Justin Stone

T'ai chi... is the wisdom of your own senses, your own mind and body together as one process.

Chungliang Al Huang

CONSIDER QIGONG

Qigong, or 'energy cultivation', is a martial art that originated in China some 3,000 years ago. Commonly associated with Taoism, qigong is said to prevent and alleviate the symptoms of a whole range of illnesses and ailments.

Aiming to help you to focus on and direct your body's essential energy (or *chi*), the gentle repetitive exercises build internal power and promote mental clarity, and the ease and fluidity of the movements make it suitable for people of all ages.

As there is such a variety of qigong styles, anyone can find a version to suit them, whatever their age or lifestyle. Whether you are seeking stress release, improved fitness or increased self-awareness, there's a form of qigong for you. The internet is a great tool for finding out more, and there are numerous books, DVDs and classes available too.

Whatever style you choose, qigong allows you to reconnect with your spirit. At its heart are three simple principles: correct your posture, deepen your breathing and open your mind.

Inner peace is found by facing life squarely, solving its problems, and delving as far beneath its surface as possible.

Peace Pilgrim

The moment one
gives close attention
to anything... it
becomes a mysterious,
awesome, indescribably
magnificent world
in itself.

Henry Miller

TRY AIKIDO

The Japanese martial art of aikido is known as 'the art of peace'. Whilst maintaining harmony between the mind and movement, students of aikido seek to defend themselves by sapping the energy of their assailant.

The discipline was developed by Morihei Ueshiba in the 1920s as a combination of jujitsu, sword and staff skills and self-defence moves. He was committed to the notion that a student should wish for peace with the universe rather than victory over their opponent, and aikido emphasises the need for a spirit of reconciliation.

Like t'ai chi, aikido is a popular activity and finding a local class should not be too challenging. As well as learning defensive skills, gaining confidence and improving your reflexes, aikido offers a spiritual dimension in which you can pursue inner peace and learn to take a step back from conflict.

LEARN TO MEDITATE

Everyone has heard of meditation, but few actually practise it, even though it is becoming more popular than ever before. It has numerous health benefits, both mental and physical, and is being used increasingly in spheres of work, leisure and even education. If you aren't already meditating, there has never been a better time to start.

Wear loose-fitting clothes and make sure you are somewhere you won't be disturbed or interrupted by telephones or tech. You do not need to sit cross-legged – just be comfortable. Using the flame of a candle as a focal point can be useful. Empty your mind, breathe normally and concentrate on the flame. A daily session of three or four minutes will suffice to start with, but, after a week or so, begin to increase the duration. You won't look back.

THE MIND CAN GO IN A THOUSAND DIRECTIONS, BUT ON THIS BEAUTIFUL PATH, I WALK IN PEACE.

Thích Nhất Hạnh

If you can attain **repose** and **calm,** believe that you have seized **happiness.**

Jeanne Julie Éléonore de Lespinasse

WORD POWER

Mantras and positive affirmations can help in all manner of situations, from problem-solving to stress relief. In Eastern cultures, words that are thought or vocalised are believed to have spiritual powers. It is no wonder, then, that mantras have been used in Buddhist meditation for centuries.

Find a word that inspires you when meditating and say or chant it, developing a rhythm that suits your natural breath. Affirmations are generally full sentences – 'I am perfect just as I am' or 'I am good enough', for example. Play around with words until you have a clutch of sentences that you can use, and alternate between them depending on your mood. Write some on sticky notes and leave them where you can see them on a daily basis to help reinforce their message.

STARGAZING MEDITATION

The night sky is used as a guide to everything from the weather to horoscopes, and spiritual people also use the stars to inspire them in meditation. On a clear night, make yourself comfortable and gaze upon the wonder of the heavens. Using individual stars as focal points, notice their shape, the brightness and the distance between the nearest neighbouring stars. Observe the limitless space above and let any anxiety and stress drift away.

You are a cosmic
flower. Om chanting
is the process of
opening the psychic
petals of that flower.

Amit Ray

DWELL ON THE BEAUTY OF LIFE. WATCH THE STARS, AND SEE YOURSELF RUNNING WITH THEM.

Marcus Aurelius

The **cosmos** is within us. We are made of **star-stuff**. We are a way for the **universe** to know itself.

Carl Sagan

COLOUR-BY-CHAKRA

Different colours are thought to have their own unique qualities and to represent different emotions. For example, blue is associated with perception, harmony and truth, and is said to connect with the 'third eye' chakra. So if you want to feel serene, wear blue.

There are seven unique chakras in the body, and they act as energy focal points. They are the crown, solar plexus, root, throat, heart, sacral and third eye. If any of the chakras become 'blocked', illnesses may occur, so it is thought best to keep them clear through meditation. When meditating, try visualising an appropriate colour wrapping itself around your body. Here are some other colours and their influences:

- Red – love, passion and anger
- Green – regeneration and fertility
- Purple – spirituality and healing
- Orange – balance, immunity and sexual potency

The soul becomes
dyed with the colour
of its thoughts.

Marcus Aurelius

COLOURS ARE THE SMILES OF NATURE.

Leigh Hunt

BE WITH TREES

Trees are said to be rich in mystical and natural energy. Studies have confirmed that walking among trees and even hugging them can help in the treatment of depression and anxiety; so if you are feeling blue, pull on your boots and make a 'trunk' call! You could try forest bathing (*Shinrin-yoku*), which was developed in Japan in the 1980s as a preventative medicine. Patients report improvements to their sense of well-being and calm from simply spending time in the forest.

Pagans set great store in the properties of different varieties of tree and believe that each species can confer its own unique benefits. For instance, if you are seeking emotional stability, sit beneath a willow; if you need strength, embrace an oak tree. A birch tree is said to represent new beginnings, while a stint in the company of a holly tree will help alleviate anger. If romance is on your mind, let yourself daydream beneath a blossoming cherry tree.

TREES ARE POEMS THAT THE EARTH WRITES UPON THE SKY.

Kahlil Gibran

In a **forest** of a
hundred thousand
trees, no two leaves are
alike, just as no two
journeys along the
same path are the same.

Paulo Coelho

SENSORY STROLLING

Balm to the soul, a sensory walk by the sea, in the woods, mountains or countryside or in peaceful parkland frees the mind, exercises the body and puts our senses through their paces. Decide on a location, make sure you're dressed for the weather and walk with the express purpose of utilising all of your senses.

Really see, hear and smell your surroundings: what do you notice? What colours delight your eyes? How many sounds can you identify? Stick your tongue out and see if you can taste, say, the salt from the sea. Touch the natural world: run sand, grass, earth or lake water through your fingers and stroke flower petals and tree bark. Pay attention to the different textures. Invigorating and centring, a sensory walk is both inspiring and restorative.

The Poetry of earth
is never dead.

John Keats

THE MOUNTAINS ARE CALLING AND I MUST GO.

John Muir

PILGRIM'S PROGRESS

If there is somewhere that you feel a spiritual connection to, and it's close enough for you to visit, make a pilgrimage. A beach, a landmark, a building – make time to visit and allow your spiritual energy to flow. If there is somewhere further afield that you have always felt a 'pull' towards, follow your instinct and consider saving for a short break or holiday there.

Even if you aren't religious, most people agree that being in a temple, mosque or church is a peaceful experience. Visit a religious building and simply sit and enjoy the surroundings and the tranquillity. Meditate or just absorb the quietude. You don't need to participate in a religious tradition to appreciate its places of worship and rituals.

I like the **silent church** before the service begins, better than any **preaching**.

Ralph Waldo Emerson

Happiness is spiritual, born of truth and love. It is unselfish; therefore it cannot exist alone, but requires all mankind to share it.

Mary Baker Eddy

GET YOGIC

Stretching the mind as well as the muscles, yoga is a wonderful way to relax and to quieten the soul. It centres us in the present and enables us to be more aware of our higher consciousness. Studies have also shown that regular 'yogis' are more adept at soothing their nervous systems and find it easier to connect with their spiritual selves. The regular practice of yoga can also lead to a number of physical benefits, such as improved heart health, greater flexibility and better posture, while also enhancing your spiritual and mental well-being.

Yoga has no religious basis and is thought to date back over 5,000 years to northern India, so it's an ancient practice that anyone can try. There are many different types of yoga – research classes near you and consider which might best suit your desire to follow a more spiritual path.

**EXERCISES
ARE LIKE PROSE,
WHEREAS YOGA
IS THE POETRY
OF MOVEMENTS.**

Amit Ray

That's why it's called
a **practice**. We have
to practise a practice if
it is to be of **value**.

Allan Lokos

RELAXING REIKI

Reiki is an established Japanese technique known for its restorative effects. The laying on of hands by a trained reiki practitioner transmits spiritual energy to the recipient threefold: physically, mentally and emotionally. One of reiki's most positive healing benefits is stress reduction and relaxation. It is also proven to improve sleep quality and acts as a key in unlocking repressed emotion. Find a local practitioner and book yourself a relaxing reiki massage.

Reiki: Calms the mind. Empowers the soul. Fills the heart with compassion.

James Deacon

FASTING FOR SPIRITUAL GROWTH

Many faiths practise fasting in order to cleanse the body and sharpen spiritual awareness. Islam, Judaism and Catholicism all have holy fasting periods, which entail going without food for a short period of time. The theory is that when we are not distracted by food – its preparation and its consumption – we are more in tune with our mind, body and spirit.

Do not attempt to fast without the approval of your doctor, and be sure to keep well hydrated. Alternatively, try 'fasting' by avoiding certain substances like alcohol, nicotine and sugar. Give your body a break and allow it to function without having to fight off the effects of mood-altering substances.

Periodic fasting can help
clear up the mind
and **strengthen** the
body and the spirit.

Ezra Taft Benson

Always laugh
when you can. It is
cheap medicine.

Lord Byron

LAUGHTER YOGA

A combination of laughter and deep-breathing yoga exercises, laughter yoga is based on the understanding that the body cannot differentiate between real and faked laughter, so the benefits to mind and body are the same: oxygenation of body and brain leads to improved physical well-being and higher energy levels. Laughter also lowers the level of stress hormones in the blood and instead releases dopamine, oxytocin, serotonin and endorphins – the 'happy' hormones.

As soap is to the
body, so laughter
is to the soul.

Yiddish proverb

CRYSTAL HEALING

Have you considered the power of crystals? If you believe in astrology, pay a visit to a holistic store for advice on which crystal is best suited to your birth sign. Otherwise, allow instinct to guide your choice, or research their properties and choose a few based on your needs and desires. For instance, rose quartz is said to strengthen relationships, onyx to give courage, and iron pyrite to ward off danger. If you travel regularly, make sure you have a piece of malachite, as this is the guardian stone for travellers. Another excellent 'voyager's' crystal is shungite, which is said to neutralise electromagnetic energy from computers and equipment such as X-ray machines and security scanning devices.

Build up your collection so that you have crystals to suit every mood or activity. Some people find that holding a crystal while meditating boosts their *chi* (life force).

BE THE ENERGY YOU WANT OTHERS TO ABSORB.

A. D. Posey

A turquoise given by a
loving hand carries
with it happiness
and good fortune.

Arabic proverb

LEARN TO CONNECT

Get into the habit of making eye contact when you speak to someone. When you look at someone properly it establishes an unspoken connection that makes communication much more honest and meaningful. The person you are in conversation with is left in no doubt that you are focused on them and that you value what they are saying.

Just as eye contact helps establish more positive connections, so too does listening properly. Practise giving people your full attention when you are in one-to-one conversation; watch how often you interrupt them with your own point of view or attempt to shout them down. By truly listening empathetically we are acknowledging the importance of another person. We also allow ourselves to hear something interesting that may even change our viewpoint. Keep your eyes and ears open and your heart and mind will follow.

THE FACE IS A PICTURE OF THE MIND AS THE EYES ARE ITS INTERPRETER.

Marcus Tullius Cicero

We have two ears and one mouth, so we should listen more than we say.

Zeno of Citium

HAVE A GRATITUDE ATTITUDE

Take regular stock of all you have to be grateful for. From the clothes on your back to the roof over your head, count all your blessings, including those we often take for granted. Start a physical gratitude list. Add to it over the course of a year and then look back at all that you have to be thankful for.

Alternatively, you could create a mental gratitude list at the end of each day, as you are preparing to sleep. Go through the day and recognise all that you had, did and encountered that deserves a 'thank you'. Both spirituality and sleep come far easier when you have a full and appreciative heart.

Gratitude **unlocks** the **fullness** of life. It turns what we have into **enough**, and more.

Melody Beattie

IF THE ONLY PRAYER YOU EVER SAID WAS THANK YOU, THAT WOULD BE ENOUGH.

Meister Eckhart

TO ERR IS HUMAN; TO FORGIVE, DIVINE

Nursing resentment is both damaging and thought-muddling. Ancient wisdom and modern-day clinical trials concur that forgiveness brings health benefits. Acts of forgiveness, while often difficult, can yield substantial rewards such as improved relationships, reduced anxiety, better heart health, a more robust immune system and lower stress levels and blood pressure.

Most importantly, forgiveness brings peace of mind. Letting go of resentment is good for clearing our spiritual pathways, and shouldn't be underestimated. Holding on to bitterness inspires negativity and makes it impossible to achieve a state of repose. The past is not there to be dwelt upon, so forgive others even when they don't deserve it: you deserve the peace.

Forgiveness is the attribute of the strong.

Mahatma Gandhi

FORGIVENESS IS NOT AN OCCASIONAL ACT – IT IS A CONSTANT ATTITUDE.

Martin Luther King Jr

LIVE IN THE NOW

The past can be useful to look back on and learn from, but for the best chance of fulfilling our spiritual potential we should endeavour to live in the present. Getting bogged down in what has gone before and that which we can't change will keep us trapped in the past – emotionally unavailable to fully experience and appreciate the present moment.

If you have a tendency to dwell on past relationships and old ills, resolve to 'look now!' rather than looking back. Exercise forgiveness and keep a forward momentum. When you catch yourself wallowing retrospectively, remind yourself gently that while it's OK to look back briefly, the past should not be stared at. It should be acknowledged, but not fixated upon.

Don't look back and ask, Why? Look ahead and ask, Why not?

Neil Patel

**BEGIN TO BE
NOW WHAT
YOU WILL BE
HEREAFTER.**

William James

BE YOUR OWN HAPPY MAGNET

To attract joy, become your own happy magnet. The laws of attraction say that if you want to feel happier, pull happiness towards you. Try seeking out those who inspire happy feelings, doing something that you know always lifts your heart, or simply looking on the things that make you smile. Whether it is watching your favourite stand-up comedian or gazing into the eyes of a loved one, live your happiness in every way that you can.

When your mood isn't especially upbeat, try faking it. There is some evidence to suggest that people who start the day in a despondent frame of mind but who make a conscious effort to act *as if* they were happy can actually lift their mood and alter their sense of spiritual well-being significantly. Happiness is also contagious, so try passing it on!

The most important thing is to enjoy your life – to be happy. It's all that matters.

Audrey Hepburn

WHEN YOU DO THINGS FROM YOUR SOUL, YOU FEEL A RIVER MOVING IN YOU, A JOY.

Rumi

SPREAD A LITTLE HAPPINESS

A small act of kindness goes a long way. To be kind is to consider someone else and their needs. To offer kindness to a stranger or to someone we don't particularly like is to touch a soul. There are countless (pleasantly surprising) benefits of extending kindness – from the developing of new friendships to the returning of favours. The greatest reward, however, is the sense of humanity and purpose that selfless giving brings.

Look for daily opportunities to be kind, whether it's just a small act or giving time, skills or money. Volunteer, donate old clothes and goods to someone who would benefit from the gift, or reach out to someone going through a hard time. Better still, become a kindness ninja! Perform an act of kindness so secretly and swiftly that the recipient has no idea who their benefactor was. Put your spare change in a vending machine as a surprise for the next person who wants to use it, or wash up any dirty mugs or dishes in your workplace kitchen. The feel-good effects of being kind are life-affirming.

A single act of
kindness throws
out roots in **all
directions,** and the
roots spring up and
make **new trees.**

Amelia Earhart

Go into the world
and do well. But more
importantly, go into the
world and do good.

Minor Myers Jr

WHO ARE YOU TO JUDGE?

Listing other people's sins and shortcomings doesn't make us saints. We also tend to judge others without complete information and therefore unfairly. In most scenarios we find ways to put people down in order to elevate ourselves, so endeavour to respect others as you would wish them to respect you. Use time that you might be tempted to spend on passing judgement on someone to work on improving yourself.

The more you can be
self-aware and honest
about yourself, the
more you can cultivate
that in other people.

Mark Pincus

A PASSION FOR PURPOSE

Be passionate! A talent, a hobby or a good cause – find something that you can throw yourself into completely and that makes your heart sing. A passion in life is a prime motivator; it keeps us learning, moving and striving. Whether it is playing the piano or raising awareness of the plight of a marginalised group, let your passion loose and see your spirits soar.

Judging is acting on
a limited knowledge.
Learn the art of
observing without
evaluating.

Pushpa Rana

My mission in life is not merely to **survive**, but to **thrive**; and to do so with some **passion**.

Maya Angelou

I WOULD
RATHER DIE OF
PASSION THAN
OF BOREDOM.

Émile Zola

CREATIVITY FOR THE SOUL

Whether it's painting a picture, colouring in, writing a poem, embroidering a cushion cover or weaving with willow, tapping into an art, craft or otherwise creative activity is good for the soul. It doesn't matter how accomplished you are; the very act of creating something is positive. Especially good for alleviating acute anxiety and obsessive thoughts, getting arty or crafty is a wonderful way to distract yourself and find a more composed state of mind.

Art enables us to
find ourselves and
lose ourselves at
the same time.

Thomas Merton

SING OUT LOUD!

Singing is proven to move our focus away from everyday concerns and towards something more spiritual. It unites people and creates positive energy, all the while soothing bodily systems and activating our natural healing process. Moreover, it is a way of expressing your soul. Try singing to yourself as you do housework, or consider joining a choir.

Creativity takes
courage.

Henri Matisse

MUSIC AND SPIRITUALITY

Keening, incantations, requiems, hymns, classical scores and modern music have all been used to express and enrich spiritual occasions. Make a playlist of music to inspire you when you are struggling to make a spiritual connection. Tap into pieces that touch you on a profound level. Don't limit yourself to any one genre – whether you find a folk song, musicals or even the theme tune to a TV show spiritually awakening, turn up the volume and let the music play on.

Words make you
think. Music makes
you feel. A song makes
you feel a thought.

Yip Harburg

WITHOUT MUSIC, LIFE WOULD BE A MISTAKE.

Friedrich Nietzsche

We are the
music makers,
And we are the
dreamers of dreams.

Arthur O'Shaughnessy

ANIMAL TRANQUILLITY

Spending time with animals can have a profoundly calming effect. They are often used to help rehabilitate people suffering from depression and nervous afflictions. Try volunteering at a local sanctuary, taking a friend's dog on a long walk or stroking a cat on your lap. It is almost impossible to feel anything other than contentment when you have the feline equivalent of a steam train purring on your knee.

Animals are such
agreeable friends – they
ask no questions, they
pass no criticisms.

George Eliot

Until one has **loved**
an animal, a part of
one's soul remains
unawakened.

Anatole France

JUST AS A CANDLE CANNOT BURN WITHOUT FIRE, MAN CANNOT LIVE WITHOUT A SPIRITUAL LIFE.

Buddhist proverb

GO BACK TO YOUR ROOTS

Take a trip down memory lane and discover your ancestors. Many cultures and spiritual traditions from around the world venerate their ancestors as an important part of their identity. By looking back at where we came from, we can get a better grasp on who we are, what we stand for and where our place is in the world. We all long to 'belong', and discovering the extent of our family trees can be a spiritual experience. Who knows? You might unearth a famous relative, or learn that you might have inherited talents for things you have never thought to try.

Talk to grandparents and older relatives about the life and work of your forebears. Ask them to talk you through photograph albums and to share their memories. If there are particularly fascinating stories to be told, take advantage of the digital age and record them – to inspire you and the generations to come.

To forget one's ancestors is to be a brook without a source, a tree without a root.

Chinese proverb

INSIGHT OCCURS WHEN, AND TO THE DEGREE THAT, ONE KNOWS ONESELF.

Andrew Schneider

EVERYDAY ENLIGHTENMENT

Try incorporating the quest for enlightenment into your daily life by making use of the numerous podcasts available on a whole range of subjects connected to spirituality. From religious services to inspirational talks and speeches, there's something out there for all tastes.

If you spend a lot of time travelling on public transport, there are various apps you can use to advance your enlightenment. Or, you could make use of the multitude of books available on all things spiritual. You may be stuck in a tunnel on the 6.15 to Waterloo, but while you're there you may as well be keeping your aura in tip-top condition or learning more about ancient sages and their timeless wisdom.

THE BEST PREPARATION FOR TOMORROW IS DOING YOUR BEST TODAY.

H. Jackson Brown Jr

Infuse your life with **action**. Don't wait for it to happen, **make it happen**. Make your own future.

Bradley Whitford

SPREAD THE LOVE!

I love you: these are, without doubt, the most welcome and warming three words we can utter. Remind those you care about of your love whenever you can. To reassure someone that they are loved is a gift. Love makes the world go round, after all.

Love is life.
All, everything
that I understand,
I understand only
because I love.
Everything is,
everything exists,
only because I love.

Leo Tolstoy

If you're interested in finding out more about our books, find us on Facebook at Summersdale Publishers and follow us on Twitter at @Summersdale.

www.summersdale.com